Musings of a Mother

Suzi Lenda

BookLeaf Publishing

India | USA | UK

Presentation by *BookLeaf Publishing*

Web: www.bookleafpub.com

E-mail: info@bookleafpub.com

ISBN: 9789358317343

First edition 2023

DEDICATION

For my darling boy, David.

I love you unconditionally - Mum xxx

ACKNOWLEDGEMENT

Karol, thank you for your unwavering support and encouragement.

PREFACE

My love for rhyming was rekindled with motherhood as I read countless rhythmic children's books to my son.

I first wrote a poem to my husband to mark father's day. I wrote as though I could see through my child's eyes. Six Brown Hens, a true except from our lives.

Milestones

How many firsts in one life?
First word, first step, first kiss.
And the firsts only you know,
First glimpse, first thought, first wish.

How much wonder and joy,
New experiences, places and things.
Unapologetic and fearless,
New friendships, relationships, flings.

A sequence of choices will shape this life,
A mistake; a new an opportunity to grow.
Find the positive, the silver linings,
Don't settle for the status quo.

To see the beauty in everything is a gift,
With clean hands and a pure heart.
Follow your instincts, have no regrets,
Your life is a masterpiece, a true work of art.

Three Big Breaths

This world can be crazy,
Too busy and loud.
Feeling overwhelmed, overstimulated,
Lost in the crowd.

Stop for a moment,
Take a pause with me.
Relax, just breathe,
One. Two. Three.

Starting to panic,
Thoughts running away.
Losing sight of reality,
Refocus to stay.

Stop for a moment,
Take a pause with me.
Relax, just breathe,
One. Two. Three.

Feeling calmer now,
Letting any tension go.
With focus on the here and now,
Just going with the flow.

Stop for a moment,
Take a pause with me.
Relax, just breathe,
One. Two. Three.

Forest Freedom

In the depths of the forest,
I am wild and free.
Exploring, foraging,
Climbing a tree.

Spotting different features,
Trailing through the dirt.
Watching every step,
Avoiding getting hurt.

Skinned knees, scrapes, and bruises,
Help shape who I am.
Hesitation, steps that falter,
A voice reminds me that I can.

Hear a noise over there,
See a shape or a shadow.
Imagination flows,
Silence falls so we can tiptoe.

Fantasy consumes us,
Another world takes over.
Goblins, monsters, creatures,
Nothing found, lack of closure.

We laugh, moving onto something else,
A fairy trail, a darkened cave, a river running
past.
Hidden paths full of possibility, endless
adventure,
Observing seasons changing and how the
colours can contrast.

Weather doesn't matter,
It's part of all the fun.
Muddy days with wellies,
Splash, jump, run.

Magical Moments

Magic all around us, belief is a choice,
Enchanted celebrations, all will rejoice.
Flashes of energy, a buzz all around,
Whimsical details to keep us spellbound.

Santa Clause and flying reindeer, deliver gifts
across the land,
Dreams are constructed by Sandman's magic
sand.
Chocolate eggs are left by the Easter Bunny,
While the Tooth Fairy tends to leave a little
money.

Miraculous, mysterious, amazing events.
Inexplicable, yes, but magic need not make
sense.
Feel the higher vibration coursing through the
air,
Hold on to the wonderment, that feeling is rare.

Say Cheese

Can I take a photo, please?
Stay still, big smile, don't forget to say cheese.

A record of what once was,
Holding onto the moment with a pause.

A memory saved, a snapshot in time,
The image captured on film, a paradigm.

Baby book, scrap book, photo book, journal,
A physical copy that feels eternal.

Only a focus on recording prevents being present,
Orchestration and posing becomes inherent.

Authentic portrayal shot with a candid frame,
Still, no record is needed for memories to remain.

Feelings at Three

I love you; I hate you.
I need you; it's not true.

All mixed up and unsure.
Range of feelings, raw and pure:

Calm, fearful, disgusted, sad,
Surprised, embarrassed, happy, mad.

Ever-changing emotions.
Deep, like the oceans.

A little voice, with a moan.
It says, 'Leave me alone'.

Yet, with a guarantee,
This is followed by 'Please, hug me'.

Lack of regulation.
This can lead to speculation.

The need to act out every feeling.
Consistency and love will lead to healing.

Park Life

A place of innocence and unfiltered joy.
Slide, swing, slide again.
Pirate ship, seesaw, hidden den.

Lessons learned and soft landings.
Trampoline, zipline, fireman's pole.
Refusal to leave, time to cajole.

Encouragement first then distraction.
Exhausted, fulfilled, a successful day.
The swing park embraces child-led play.

Futile Lies of Childhood

I tell lies and I don't know why.
I do it with ease, I don't even try.

I am small and uncertain and sometimes afraid.
It's hard to keep up and maintain the charade.

I tell lies and I don't know why.
Maybe I'm lost or lonely or shy.

I do know the difference between right and
wrong.
Deep down, I think, I just want to belong.

I tell lies and I don't know why,
The limit can be as high as the sky.

Sometimes I'm a hero, sometimes I'm a fool,
Sometimes I pretend to break every rule.

I tell lies and I don't know why,
Some are bold while others simply imply.

I am trying to improve and be honest and kind.
Having someone to trust helps me feel realigned.

I don't want to tell lies, that I do know.
I want to be truthful, develop and grow.

Speaking openly with others will help on this
road.
Trusted family and friends can help to unload.

I used to tell lies and now I know why,
The truth brings a little tear to my eye.

I don't need to cover mistakes or tell people a
story.
I don't need to pretend or make up false glory.

I used to tell lies and now I know why,
No one asked about issues that might underlie.

True friendship, love, and belonging are key,
To feel valued and cherished for being me.

I used to tell lies and now I know why,
I didn't appreciate all that is I.

You've helped me to see that I am enough.
I don't need to tell lies, I am strong and I'm
tough.

I used to tell lies but that was before,
Now I know who I am, I don't need to be more.

Jurassic Garden

There's a dino in my garden, he's out there all
the time.
At first, I was uncertain but now I think of him
as mine.

Dino is a T-Rex, he's big, green, and mean.
I would be quite frightened if he ever made a
scene.

Dino's arms are tiny, but he has a mighty roar.
I don't think he ever sleeps; I've never heard
him snore.

Perched in the arch of the apple tree, Dino stays
all day and night.
On guard, he would frighten off the bad guys
with his snarl and a bite.

I like to feed him apples, he seems to like them
best.
When I give him sticks or dirt or stones, he is
not impressed.

One day I will lose interest, I won't notice Dino
by the tree.

For now, a nod of thanks to Dino as he keeps
watch over me.

13

Passage of Time

Another year passes,
Where does the time go?
It's both a joy and a heartache,
Watching you grow.

Moments and memories treasured.
Yet, lives evolve, and the progression is fast.
With each stage cherished,
Change determines it, nothing can last.

The time will come when you need me no more.
In good health, this will be at your discretion.
With no guarantees, know my love does not
falter.
If you only have me in spirit, please remember
this lesson:

Live greatly my darling,
Just be who you are.
I will love you always,
My shining star.

Uninfluenced

15

Whether you have or have not,
Happiness, cannot be bought.

Possessions and things do not form your worth,
This was instilled in you from birth.

Followers and likes are nice in theory,
Validation through others will leave you weary.

Social media will only show a highlight reel,
It should never influence how you feel.

With nothing to prove to those that count,
Know that living your truth is paramount.

Life Lessons

Lessons unfold throughout this life,
Basic skills to conquer without stress or strife.

How to swim, skate and ride a bike,
Accepting people and things that you do or don't
like.

Saving energy for all that brings deep joy,
How to look after and treasure a precious toy.

Learning the lyrics to a favourite song,
The importance of history and where you come
from.

As we get older, the lessons don't end,
How to cook, clean, make and mend.

Tough decisions, effectively managing time,
Challenging prospects of the corporate climb.

Lessons in love and inevitable loss,
How to be your own person, a leader, a boss.

Lean into the learning, it's all meant to be,
Be gracious, be open, be honest, be free.

Harsh World

Poverty, conflict, mass unrest,
Infection enforcing house arrest.

It's a challenge to see the light through the dark,
When the future looks so bleak and stark.

Noone imagined a pandemic in this day and age
Proceeding this, it was wars that would rage.

Climate crisis causing global warming,
Fires and floods, take heed of the warning.

Cancel culture and the woke world uprising,
Political movement is not surprising.

Always remember the foundations of right and
wrong,
When faced with adversity, know you are strong.

On Track

Other people always have opinions,
Yet their views are none of your business.
Do not be discouraged and do not fret,
We all have strength and greatness within us.

Conforming would be a mistake,
A loss of self, damaging free will.
Independence and personal growth
Focus on values, learn a new skill.

Do what you're good at,
Love what you do.
Find joy in everyday things,
To your purpose stay true.

Keep your standards high,
You deserve the best.
Your worth is immeasurable,
Don't settle for less.

Beach Days

Barefoot in the sand,
Toes dip into the sea.
Living near the coast,
How lucky are we?

Saltwater and sea air,
Sandcastles and shells.
Digging for treasure,
Surfing the swells.

Relaxing, unwinding,
The calm in the storm.
Ice cream and candyfloss,
Perfect place when it's warm.

Big Picture

Devices lose signal,
The trees are blamed.
Technology can be fickle,
Frustration needs tamed.

See the big picture,
Not the one on small screens.
Life can be richer,
And, clearer than it seems.

Photosynthesis, essential,
Trees filling our lungs.
Time and space, existential,
Watch all it becomes.

Spend time in nature,
Ground with the land.
Reflect on behaviour,
Extend a helping hand.

Fresh air and sunlight,
Can alter a mood.
Abundance in sight,
Through peace, and gratitude.

Pour It Out

Never bottle anything up,
Pressurised vessels can erupt.

Pour everything out, nothing to hide,
Don't let things fester deep inside.

Something to say is better said,
This minimises the risk of being misread.

Showing vulnerability is always hard,
Be selective but try to let down your guard.

Always be honest and have no shame,
Healthy relationships are yours to claim.

Disregard any stereotype or perceived gender
role,
Everyone benefits from baring their soul.

Learn to express your thoughts, hopes and fears,
This will be extremely useful throughout the
years.

Dream On

Good manners and grace can go a long way,
Small Acts of kindness will make someone's
day.

Values and morals guide each decision,
Belief and faith will shape every vision.

Mistakes are expected, par for the course,
Resilience will act as a driving force.

Reach for the biggest dream you hold dear,
Perseverance is key, there is nothing to fear.

Six Brown Hens

My Dad rescued six brown hens from a factory
farm.
He built them a house to keep them safe from
harm.

The hens are big and fluffy, feathers soft like
snow.
They follow me in the garden, wherever I go.

We run together and they peck at my toes.
If I get too close, they'll even peck at my nose.

The hens are all friends, they stick together.
They like to explore, no matter the weather.

The hens would rather have a mud bath than
splash in the puddles.
My Mum reminds me to be gentle when I give
them big cuddles.

I play with the hens often and, for that, I'm glad.
I love our hens, they're the best; thank you, Dad.

A Mother's Love

In its purest configuration,
With only one expectation.
A mother's love and adoration,
Never lost in translation.

In success and failure,
Affection does not wane.
Regardless of behaviour,
A mother's love remains the same.

A love so great,
Willingness to sacrifice all.
There is no debate,
True love and enthral.

Disagreement or dispute
Will not change a thing.
Open to talk or troubleshoot,
A love to override anything.

A love like no other,
Hard to comprehend.
The love of a mother,
Has no end.

Routine Recap

What was the best bit of your day?
What follows is a recap of routines, adventures,
tall tales, interactions and sentiment.
The day through your eyes is precious,
Having insight into your world is enchanting;
your self-expression is excellent.

I love you
    I love you

I love you more
    I love you more

I love you the most
    I love you the most

I love you to the moon and back
    I love you to the moon and back

You're my little angel
    You're my big angel

I'm so proud of you
    I'm so proud of you

Sweet dreams, my darling boy.